I0411983

HOW TO COME OUT OF DEBT

5 PRACTICAL APPROACHES TO COME OUT OF DEBT AND RECLAIM YOUR FINANCIAL FUTURE

BY

JOHN C. DAVIDSON

TABLE OF CONTENT

INTRODUCTION

For millions of people and families, debt has become an all-too-common companion in a world where financial strains seem to be expanding at an exponential rate. Dreams of financial security and independence can seem further away as a result of increasing credit card debt, unpaid bills, and looming loan payments. But there is hope and a way out of this difficult situation, so do not be alarmed. It's a pleasure to have you here at "How to Come Out of Debt: A Practical Approach to Reclaim Your Financial Future."

This book offers a blueprint to financial freedom, a lighthouse of hope for anyone feeling bound by their present financial situation, and a guiding light in the darkness of debt. It aims to empower readers to liberate themselves from the chains of debt and reclaim control over their financial future by offering a realistic and concrete method.

"How to Come Out of Debt" takes readers on a transformational journey by drawing on the combined knowledge of God's word, financial professionals, real-life success stories, and time-tested solutions. It starts with addressing the underlying causes of debt, busting myths about money management, and clearing up common misconceptions that frequently get in the way of progress. From then, it gradually guides readers towards gaining a thorough awareness of their financial condition and the variables that affect their level of debt.

The core of this book is its practical advice and tried-and-true techniques for overcoming debt. Readers will learn how to make a personalized debt payback plan, set a reasonable budget, and develop sound financial practices through a series of practical exercises and interactive tools. Beyond that, it explores the art of bargaining with creditors, looks at debt consolidation options, and uses practical techniques to prevent getting sucked back into the debt cycle.

But achieving financial freedom requires adopting a new mindset that values long-term financial sustainability and prosperity, not merely getting rid of debt. This book also offers advice on how to set up an emergency fund, make prudent investments, and make future financial plans.

Even while the path to financial freedom is not simple, it is unquestionably worthy. With "How to Come Out of Debt," readers may set out on this journey with the knowledge and confidence to take back control of their money and create a brighter, more prosperous future.

Turn the page now to start the transition if you're prepared to free yourself from debt's stranglehold and pave the way to financial independence. Through the pages of this book, arm yourself with information, prepare yourself with tactics, and set out on a road of emancipation. Let's go forward into a future free of debt, where opportunities abound and ambitions are attainable. We will defeat debt collectively, recover our financial future, and create a strong and prosperous financial life.

CHAPTER ONE

UNDERSTANDING THE TOTALITY OF

DEBT

Debt has an impact on the lives of people, corporations, and entire countries. It is like a complex web that is woven into the fabric of our contemporary civilization. It is both a potent force for advancement and a weight that might limit goals. To unravel the subtleties that lie beyond debt's surface and reveal its complicated nature and wide-ranging effects, it is necessary to comprehend debt in its entirety. In this investigation, we set out on a quest to demystify debt in order to gather knowledge about its causes, effects on economies, and significant impact on the lives of countless people.

WHAT IS DEBT?

Debt is a phrase used in finance to describe an obligation or liability owed by one party—the debtor—to another—the creditor. It is a representation of the sum of money or value that the debtor owes to the creditor, usually as a result of borrowing money or making purchases of goods and services on credit. A debt is created when a person, company, or government borrows money or purchases products or services on credit. The parameters of repayment, such as the sum owed, the interest rate (if applicable), and the payback schedule, are outlined in a contract that is created between the debtor and the creditor.

According to Merriam Webster dictionary, DEBT is a state of being under obligation to pay or repay someone or something in return for something received : a state of owing.

But the bible teaches comprehensively according to the book of Romans 13:8, saying "Owe no man". There are many bible references about DEBT being owed, but specifically we'll be considering a man who served God faithful before he died according to 1 Kings 4:1. This shows that even a Christian can be indebted but that is not the will of God.

WHO IS A DEBTOR?

A debtor is a person, company, or other entity that owes money or is obligated financially to the creditor. Simply put, a debtor is someone who has borrowed money, purchased products or services on credit, or signed a contract entitling them to make payments in the future.

A debtor can be:

INDIVIDUAL: A person can incur debt by taking out personal loans, mortgages, or credit card balances from a bank or other financial organization. A person also becomes a debtor to the respective vendors or service providers if they do not make payment for the goods or services they have received.

BUSINESS: Businesses frequently take on debt to fund their operations, grow their businesses, or buy the tools and resources they need. This can entail signing trade credit agreements with suppliers, securing bank loans, or issuing bonds.

GOVERNMENT: When governments borrow money to pay for public initiatives, the construction of infrastructure, or to close budget gaps, they are also considered debtors. Treasury bonds and other securities are issued by governments to attract capital from investors.

A legal contract or agreement that specifies the parameters of the debt, such as the principal amount borrowed, the interest rate (if applicable), the repayment schedule, and any other particular conditions, forms the basis of the debtor-creditor relationship. The contract's provisions must be followed by the debtor, who must pay the creditor on schedule and in full up until that point.

For debtors to avoid fines, retain their creditworthiness, and avoid the buildup of excessive debt that could result in financial troubles, it is crucial that they handle their financial commitments responsibly by making sure they pay their bills on time and on schedule.

THE VARIOUS FORMS OF DEBT

Understanding the different varieties of debt is crucial because they can have varied effects on both the debtor and the creditor. Debt can take many different forms. Here are a few examples of typical debts:

CONSUMER DEBT: People acquire this kind of debt to cover personal expenses. It contains:

Debt incurred as a result of delinquent balances and purchases made with credit cards.

Personal loans are sums of money lent for one's own use from banks, credit unions, or online lenders.

Student loans are loans taken out to pay for schooling and associated costs.

Auto loans: Debt taken out to buy an automobile that is frequently secured by the car itself.

Debt from mortgages: A mortgage is a loan used to buy real estate, typically a home. The asset is used as security for the debt, which is paid off over a long period of time through regular mortgage payments.

CORPORATE DEBT: To fund operations, expansion, or investment in new initiatives, businesses may incur numerous types of debt. Typical forms of business debt include:

CORPORATE BONDS: Debt securities that businesses issue to raise money from investors and make regular interest payments and principal repayments at maturity.

Loans taken out by a corporation to cover its financing needs from banks or other financial organizations.

Lines of Credit: A revolving credit line that companies can draw from as needed; frequently utilized for pressing needs relating to working capital.

GOVERNMENT DEBT: Local, state, and federal governments may take on debt to pay for infrastructure improvements, public projects, and other costs. Typically, the government issues debt through:

TREASURY BONDS: Long-term debt securities with set interest rates and maturities of several years to decades that are issued by governments.

TREASURY BILLS (T-BILLS): Short-term debt instruments that typically have maturities between a few days and a year.

Intermediate-term debt instruments with maturities in between Treasury Bonds and T-Bills are known as Treasury Notes.

SECURED DEBT: Some loans have collateral backing that the creditor may seize if the borrower defaults on the repayment plan. Examples comprise:

Loans that are secured by certain assets, such as a house (a mortgage) or a car (an auto loan), are referred to as secured loans.

PAWN SHOP LOANS: These are short-term loans where the collateral is valuable goods.

Unsecured Debt: Unsecured debt depends only on the creditworthiness of the borrower and does not require any type of security. Common illustrations include:

CREDIT CARD DEBT: Unsecured debt accumulated as a result of purchases made with credit cards and outstanding amounts.

SIGNATURE LOANS: Unsecured loans given based only on the borrower's income and credit history.

Every type of debt has its own terms, interest rates, and repayment plans. Individuals and corporations can manage their financial commitments responsibly and make educated financial decisions by being aware of the many types of debt.

CHAPTER TWO

PEOPLE AND DEBT

Debt and people have a complicated and diverse relationship that affects people from all socioeconomic origins and areas of life. Debt may be a potent weapon that helps people accomplish their objectives, invest in their education, buy houses, and launch businesses. Debt, however, can grow to be a heavy weight if it is not well handled, creating anxiety and uncertainty over money.

The relationship between people and debt has the following important components:

Borrowing and Financial Possibilities: People who are in debt have access to options they might not otherwise have. For instance, student loans can help people who cannot afford the upfront expenditures of higher education, and mortgages allow people to buy homes and gradually create wealth. Similarly, small company loans can assist entrepreneurs in converting their concepts into profitable businesses.

Consumer Debt: Personal loans and credit card debt are two major forms of consumer debt. It might be helpful for handling emergencies or making necessary expenditures. High interest rates and excessive expenditure, however, might result in debt buildup and money problems.

Financial Stress: When people find it difficult to take on their responsibilities, debt can lead to a great deal of stress and anxiety for them. Debt load can have an impact on one's general well-being, relationships, and mental health.

Credit Scores and Creditworthiness: An individual's credit score, which is an important consideration when asking for loans or other types of credit, can be positively impacted by appropriately managing debt. Better financial opportunities and more favorable interest rates can result from having a high credit score.

Debt traps: Some people may become mired in debt cycles, especially if they take out expensive payday loans or use predatory lending techniques. Escaping these debt traps can be difficult and may require support and financial education.

Debt and Financial Literacy: Problems with debt can be exacerbated by a lack of financial literacy. There are many people who might not fully comprehend the conditions of their loans, the ramifications of high interest rates, or how to make a budget and manage their money wisely.

Debt and Socioeconomic disparity: Those with limited access to finance may find it difficult to pursue educational or business opportunities, which can increase socioeconomic disparity.

Debt Relief and Bankruptcy: In situations of severe debt, people may look for debt relief by consolidating their debt, negotiating with their creditors, or, in the worst cases, declaring bankruptcy.

In general, cautious thought and sound money management are needed when dealing with the interaction between people and debt. Individuals can be empowered to make informed decisions and avoid falling into the trap of unmanageable debt by understanding the conditions of loans, living within one's means, and pursuing financial education. Achieving long-term financial well-being requires striking a balance between using debt to leverage opportunities and upholding financial stability.

POSSIBLE CAUSES OF DEBT

Understanding the probable causes of debt is crucial for managing one's money properly because debt can result from a variety of variables and situations. Here are a few typical debt-related causes:

UNEXPECTED EVENTS: Unexpected occurrences like medical emergencies, auto repairs, or house maintenance might result in unforeseen costs. If people don't have enough emergency savings or insurance, they might use credit cards or loans to pay for these expenses.

LIVING BEYOND MEANS: Excessive spending and living above one's means can swiftly result in debt accumulation. Credit card overuse without a strategy for paying off the sums in full can lead to exorbitant interest rates and a vicious cycle of debt. For instance, someone who loves tropical vacations without considering their current financial state but decides to go ahead because they love pleasure that will lead to pressure in the future. Also window shopping can be a form of living beyond mean. It is always important to have a list of present needs before going to the store for shopping.

JOB LOSS OR INCOME REDUCTION: A rapid change in work status or a considerable drop in income might cause financial instability. People who don't have enough savings may turn to borrowing to cover living costs during these trying times. Those who lived with a daily budget of $200 while working with an oil company as senior staff should reasonably understand that they should reduce daily expenses when the contract is terminated.

STUDENT LOANS: In order to pay for tuition, fees, and living expenses while pursuing a higher education, student loans are frequently obtained. While investing in one's future through education, student loans can result in heavy debt loads, especially if graduates have trouble obtaining well-paying professions. At this point I'll suggest that a student with first degree should get a good paying job that will help to save enough money for those intending to further get a masters or doctorate degree, to avoid being indebted without a befitting job.

MEDICAL EXPENSES: Even with insurance coverage, healthcare costs can be high. In certain circumstances, mounting medical debt forces people to look for financial aid through loans or payment arrangements.

Credit Card Debt: Due to compound interest rates, improper use of credit cards, making just minimum payments, and holding high amounts can cause credit card debt to grow quickly.

Easy Access to Credit: Because credit cards, personal loans, and other borrowing options are readily available, some people may incur debt before carefully examining their ability to repay it. Some people just enjoy borrowing because they have access to loans and it's one easy trap to being indebted.

FINANCIAL ILLITERACY: Making poor financial decisions and building up unmanageable debt can result from a lack of understanding of finances and how debt works.

High housing expenditures, such as rent or mortgage payments, can take a sizable chunk out of a person's income, leaving less money for other essentials and possibly pushing them into credit use. A wise man said that "life is in phases and men are in sizes" Please live your size to avoid debt

ADVERTISING AND CONSUMERISM: Impulsive spending and the use of credit to finance pointless purchases can be influenced by advertising and societal pressure to continuously improve goods. Not every product advertised on TV or social media is for you. Please take note

BUSINESS EXPENSES: Businesses and entrepreneurs may take on debt to finance operations, growth, or investments. While using business debt strategically, poor management or a difficult economic climate might cause financial difficulties.

LEGAL PROBLEMS: People may find it difficult to manage unforeseen financial pressures without turning to debt when faced with legal difficulties, such as litigation or fines.

Addressing and reducing the causes of debt demands proactive financial planning, frugal spending, and establishing a solid financial literacy foundation. People who want to efficiently manage their debt and work towards long-term financial stability can benefit by developing a budget, setting aside money for emergencies, and researching different debt repayment options.

STAGES OF DEBT

The numerous phases that people or corporations may experience as they accrue and manage debt are referred to as the "stages of debt." Depending on the situation and the sort of debt involved, these stages can change. The typical stages of debt are as follows:

Debt accumulation marks the start of the process. This often happens when people or corporations take out loans, use credit cards, mortgages, or other kinds of credit to borrow money or take on debt. The debt is acquired to pay for particular requirements, expenditures, or investments.

DEBT UTILIZATION: In this stage, individuals or businesses utilize the borrowed funds for their intended purposes. For example, a person might use a student loan to pay for tuition, while a business may use a loan to purchase new equipment. It is therefore important to use every loan for the very purpose which was taken to avoid regret and depression during repayment.

REPAYMENT INITIATION: The repayment stage begins when the borrower is required to start making payments towards the debt. Depending on the terms of the loan or credit agreement, repayment may start immediately after borrowing or at a later specified date. It's wrong not to repay debts. Psalm 37:21 says, "The wicked borrow but do not pay back." So it is important you have a repayment plan so that God will not consider you a wicked person and that will incur some challenges in a person's life because God is angry with the wicked everyday according to the bible book of Psalms 7:11

REGULAR REPAYMENT: This stage involves the ongoing, regular repayment of the debt according to the agreed-upon schedule. Borrowers make periodic payments, such as monthly installments, to gradually reduce the outstanding debt balance.

MANAGEMENT OF DEBT OBLIGATIONS: As the debt repayment progresses, borrowers must manage their debt obligations within their budget and financial capabilities. This stage may involve adjusting spending habits and prioritizing debt payments to ensure timely repayments.

DEBT REDUCTION: The stage of debt reduction occurs as borrowers steadily decrease the outstanding balance of their debts through regular payments. With each payment, the debt becomes smaller, and the borrower moves closer to becoming debt-free.

COMPLETION OF DEBT REPAYMENT: This is the final stage, where the borrower successfully repays the entire debt amount, fulfilling their financial obligation to the creditor. Completing debt repayment marks the achievement of becoming debt-free.

It's important to note that these stages may not apply to all types of debt uniformly. For example, student loans might have different repayment terms compared to credit card debt or a mortgage. Additionally, the stages may vary depending on the borrower's financial circumstances and the ability to meet the repayment schedule.

Throughout the stages of debt, responsible financial management, budgeting, and timely payments are crucial to avoiding excessive debt accumulation and maintaining a healthy financial standing. Being proactive in managing debt can help individuals or businesses navigate these stages successfully and achieve long-term financial stability.

WHY PEOPLE GO INTO DEBT

People go into debt for various reasons, and the decision to borrow money or incur financial obligations is often influenced by specific circumstances and financial needs.

I have heard people make foolish statements that have kept them indebted for many years because they lack understanding. Most of those sayings are: "I have relations abroad that usually send me money during Christmas or whenever I call them and explain my need". Another instance is a friend who took a loan and said his brother is a politician and in government therefore he'll either send money or give him an appointment that will place him in a money well. These people forget that everyone has their challenges and when they are pressed they'll not take anyone's call until they are free. Please be wise.

Here are some foolish reasons why people may go into debt:

DESIRE FOR INSTANT FULFILLMENT:

Individuals who want to keep up with society trends and get rapid fulfillment may overspend and incur debt. Why would someone be living in a hotel for a long period of two months with the belief that an inheritance will be given to him in the nearest future. Also considering a case of someone who loves women to a fault that He can even borrow money to pay for hotel bills, buy food and drinks for weeks just because of sex that nobody has been given an award since the world began. Another instance is someone who lives a fake life by taking a flight instead of going to the train station. There are too many instances to be considered, but if you belong to any of these foolish categories please you have to adjust so you don't become a debtor for life.

Lack of Savings: When faced with unforeseen costs or financial difficulties, people may be forced to take on debt due to a lack of savings or the absence of an emergency fund. I know a lot of people who worked with multinationals as intercontinental staff but today they are very broke because they spent money lavishly without saving, including tongue speaking Christians. Even God almighty respects the principle of saving, which was why when Elijah cried to Him that Israel has killed all the prophets and that he was the only one left, God simply told him that He has reserved for Himself 7000 prophets that have not bowed their knee to Baal. From the bible book of 1 Kings 19:18. With this scripture we see that having a savings plan is important for the future.

Each person's financial situation is different, and a variety of circumstances might have an impact on whether or not they decide to take on debt. To keep debt manageable and prevent financial misery, responsible financial management is vital. This includes setting up a budget, saving money, and comprehending the terms of loans.

CHAPTER THREE
HOW TO COME OUT OF DEBT

Discipline, strategic planning, and proactive financial management are all necessary for debt relief. While it could take some time and effort, doing the following actions can help people or organizations take back control of their money and strive towards debt freedom:

ASSESS YOUR DEBT SITUATION: Begin by carefully examining your debts. List each debt's total outstanding balance, interest rate, required minimum payment, and due date. Having a thorough understanding of all of your financial commitments is essential for developing a debt repayment plan.

MAKE A BUDGET: Create a monthly budget that takes into account your income, expenses, and debt repayments. Set aside a percentage of your salary for debt repayment while making sure you can pay for your basic needs and accumulate an emergency fund to prevent having to use credit to meet unforeseen expenses.

DEBT PRIORITIZATION: Think about concentrating on one of these two well-liked debt repayment methods:

DEBT SNOWBALL: Pay off debts in sequence of decreasing balance, starting with the smallest. When you successfully pay off minor obligations, you will feel psychologically motivated to pay off larger bills since you will have more money available to do so.

DEBT AVALANCHE: Sort your debts according to their interest rates, paying the most interest ones off first. The overall amount of interest paid over time is reduced by this strategy.

Talk to your creditors about negotiating better conditions for repayment, lower interest rates, or even debt settlement possibilities if you are experiencing financial difficulty. Many creditors are eager to negotiate with those who approach their obligations in a proactive manner.

AVOID TAKING ON NEW DEBT: Put a temporary stop to new borrowing until your existing debts are under control. While attempting to become debt-free, resist the urge to take on more debt.

INCREASED INCOME: Look for ways to boost your income, such as getting a side gig, working as a freelancer, or selling things you no longer need. Debt repayment can be done right away with the extra money.

REDUCE UNNECESSARY EXPENSES: Examine your spending patterns to find places where you might reduce unneeded costs. Use the money you've saved to pay off debt.

Debt consolidation may result in cheaper interest rates and a simpler repayment schedule. Consider these options if they can help you. Examples include personal loans and credit cards with balance transfers. Be cautious, though, and make sure the consolidation option will be to your long-term advantage.

CONSULT A PROFESSIONAL: If you're having trouble managing your bills or coming up with a repayment plan, you might want to consult a financial advisor or a credit counseling agency. They are able to offer tailored support and direction.

MAINTAIN DEDICATION AND PERSISTENCE: Reducing debt is a journey that calls for commitment and perseverance. Celebrate your advancements as you go along and keep your attention on your objective of debt freedom.

Though getting out of debt may take some time, you can take charge of your finances and strive towards a more stable and debt-free future with commitment and self-discipline.

HOW I CAME OUT OF DEBT

I have realized from my experiences over the years that borrowing can be addictive and that debt is a strategy from the pit of hell to keep a believer poor and unrest.

In 2003 I was managing my sister's business, who was schooling outside the States, and I wasn't having my personal money because she wasn't paying me, although my feeding and daily expenses were from the business and I wasn't getting enough for myself. So, I decided to get a job from a friend who asked me to come over to his state where he believed I'll have better chances of getting a job considering that I just have a high school diploma, so I called my sister and decided to leave. Before I left I took a $15 loan from a friend believing to pay back as soon as I get a job that could pay me at least $60 monthly but I was disappointed after spending the money i had in me in a strange land without getting a job after waiting for 3 weeks, so I returned back home now indebted of $15.

Long story short, I borrowed another $75 so i can repay the $15 and then start a business with the remaining $60 but the money i tried the more I kept getting into debt and when i realized 7 years later, I was already owing $500 because i was borrowing and repaying, which is simple digging a pit to cover a pit, there'll still be a pit to be covered. I was embarrassed publicly by microfinance banks calling me a criminal and other names.

Finally, when I realized I was called into ministry to preach the gospel of JESUS nine years later, I knew I couldn't get started being indebted so I had to sit down with God's word (the bible) to discover how to come out of debt. And at last I was instructed by the Holy Spirit while meditating, to go into a covenant with God for Him to clear my debts because I couldn't do it myself over the years. Immediately I obeyed, GOD stepped in and my financial liberty was established. Today I preach the gospel freely as a multi-millionaire. This might not be the same for you but in the next chapter I'll show you the 5 practical approaches that can bring you out of debt based on God's word. It has worked for me and many others and I believe if you put these actionable steps that I'll show you in this book, you'll be on your way to financial freedom.

HOW TO LIVE DEBT FREE

With careful planning, sound financial practices, and a commitment to handling your money well, living debt-free is a goal that is doable. These actions will assist you in living debt-free:

Make a Budget: Create a thorough budget that details your income, costs, and savings objectives. You may reduce your spending and put more money towards savings and debt repayment by understanding where your money is going. This action is very important because spending money without proper budgeting is one of the easiest ways people go into debt. Knowing your monthly and overall monthly expenses will help you budget well.

Prioritize paying off your existing obligations by paying them off first. To systematically pay off debts one by one, use the debt repayment techniques outlined previously, such as the debt snowball or debt avalanche method. Some people will be indebted and still spend money on things that doesn't help them come out of debt, so it's important you prioritize coming out of debt so you can be free completely.

Create an Emergency Fund: Create a savings account with enough money in it to cover three to six months' worth of expenses. If you have this safety net, you can avoid using credit cards or loans to cover unforeseen financial losses. For instance, some men have made God look so unkind to them. A married man whose wife is pregnant should not pretend he doesn't know that a delivery day will come. This is exactly why pregnancy is for 9 months so the man can have enough time to save and plan to avoid running helter scatter when the wife is due.

After you have paid off your current bills, make a commitment to living within your means and staying out of debt. Pay attention to your expenditures and limit your purchases to what your present income will allow. The hard truth is that until you make up your mind to live debt free you cannot come out of debt.

Save for Major Purchases: Start saving early rather than waiting until you need credit to make major purchases. With this strategy, you'll be able to make cash payments without accruing loan interest. If you have a child who'd be in the university in 12 months, it will be very wise to open a separate savings account ahead to avoid excuses that will frustrate you and the child.

Reduce Unnecessary Expenses: Examine your spending patterns to find places where you might reduce unneeded costs. Use the money you save to increase your savings and your investment portfolio. I have said this before, you cannot have a house and still live in a hotel in the same city, that's another definition of madness. Or you like driving to visit friends in other cities because you are looking for where things are happening instead of making things happen around you and save the cost of gas for work and other reasonable adventures. Not like you won't visit friend, but it shouldn't be always

Avoid using credit cards wherever possible and instead opt to utilize cash or debit cards for purchases. This behavior will stop you from taking on additional credit card debt.

Invest Wisely: As soon as you are debt-free and have amassed an emergency fund, think about putting your money in things that can yield returns over time, such as stocks, mutual funds, or retirement accounts. This investment plan will help and support you in the long run.

Seek Professional Financial Advice: If you need help with long-term financial planning or find it difficult to manage your finances, you might want to speak with a financial counselor. They can offer you personalized guidance based on your unique objectives and situation.

Maintain Your Commitment and Discipline: Living debt-free calls for perseverance and self-control. Maintain your commitment to your financial objectives, monitor your development, and fend against the need to overspend or take on additional debt.

Keep in mind that getting to a debt-free lifestyle is a journey, and it could take some time. Be kind to yourself and remember to recognize your progress along the way. You can live a more financially secure and debt-free life by forming wise financial habits and making well-informed choices.

CHAPTER FOUR

5 PRACTICAL APPROACHES

In the previous chapter we discussed the natural and possible ways of how anyone can come out of debt logically, but I have also observed based on my personal experience and also from others that some debts are beyond human control, which is why these 5 practical approaches are revealed from (2 Kings 4:1-7) to establish our financial liberty forever.

Getting the supernatural wisdom from God's word through the bible which is a source of all ultimate solutions to life's problems, we'll see how anyone can come out of debt whether it was inherited, attracted, manipulated from the pit of hell or ignorantly incurred.

First of all you must understand that God wants you to live debt free because (3 John 2) He wants you to prosper therefore you have to believe right now that God is able to bring you out of debt no matter how much or how long you have been in that state.

Below are the 5 practical approaches that have been tested and proven from the bible and also by hundreds of people who have taken these steps.

APPROACH GOD WITH HUMILITY AND TRUTH (2 KINGS 4:1):

A lot of people live arrogant life towards others and even before God almighty and because of that they don't get help from

God because God resists the proud (James 4:6) The reason why you should approach God concerning your case is because God is willing to hear you and reason with you and to give you every possible solution as fast as possible (Isaiah 1:18) In this scripture God said come now!. This is an indication He wants to attend to you now. You can approach God in prayer, via his word or through anointed men ordained by God.

Looking at God's word from the bible book of (2 Kings 4:1) A widow cried to a man of God because of the debt incurred by her late husband who served God faithfully. But then it got to a point where she couldn't handle it because her sons were to be taken so she approached God through a prophet. You too can approach God to be free completely from debt.

HAVE A SPECIFIC DESIRE OF WHAT YOU WANT GOD TO DO FOR YOU (2 KINGS 4:2A):

Some people who are indebted still cannot state specifically what they want God to do for them. We see many instances in the bible where Jesus asked people what they want, that is because God likes us to be specific in our approach and dealings with Him. In the scripture above, the prophet asked the woman what she'd like him to do for her. At this point some people will say I want to get a job, of course getting a job is good but I have seen people working with multinational companies who are still indebted. So, getting a job is not an ultimate means of coming out of debt. Others might even tell God to give them a capital for business so they can make profit to repay their loans but that also may not solve the problem because the person might not have the right business psychology to run the business because of the debt.

At this point I believe the woman cried out with tears in her eyes and said "please sir i want the debt to be cleared" that's exactly how to approach God. Let God be the one to decide which strategy is better for you, whether to get a job, a business or whether He'll miraculously touch the heart of the creditor to cancel it which is also very possible with God because He alone can make it happen. Have a specific desire of what you want God to do for you.

WHAT DO YOU HAVE? (2 KINGS 4:2B):

Understand that whenever a material miracle is needed, there must be a material point of contact. In my case I had to dedicate by covenant all the properties i inherited from my late biological father which was what i had so that GOD will use it as a point of contact for my miracle. So also this woman was asked by the prophet what she has because the principle cannot change and the scriptures cannot be broken. Even God almighty when he needed to recover His sons and daughters after the fall of Adam had to give His only begotten Son Jesus to get us back. Another example was Abraham who God asked to give Isaac which he did and God saw that from Abraham's heart Isaac had already died because he wanted to be the father of many nations. Jesus also came on the scene in a marriage where the material point of contact of getting a wine was to fetch water as a material point of contact. Again when He fed the 5000 men excluding women and children he used the available 5 loaves of bread and 2 fishes. So you see at this point you must have something that God will bless and multiply to bring you out of debt. Whether food or money no matter how small, there must be something you have. In the case of the woman who approached God through the prophet, she had a pot of oil and that was where her miracle of debt free began.

PAY ATTENTION TO EVERY INSTRUCTIONS AND DIRECTION THAT WILL BE GIVEN BY GOD VIA

HIS WORD, THROUGH A PROPHET OR BY THE HOLY SPIRIT (2 KINGS 4:3-4): A lot of people have failed in various endeavors because they did not pay close attention to instructions. When it comes to dealing with God it is always important to pay quality attention because spiritual things are very powerful. If you do it 99% it will not work because God is a God of details. It doesn't matter if you are a professor or one of the world's proven economists, you must follow God's instructions no matter how ridiculous otherwise you'll not have the result you desire.

TAKE HEED TO DO EXACTLY WHAT WILL BE INSTRUCTED PROMPTLY AND

FAITHFULLY (2 KINGS 4:5-6): Every delayed obedience in the kingdom of God is regarded as disobedience. One of the reasons why Abraham in the bible was outstanding was because he acted promptly on every instruction from God even when it doesn't seem convenient. A lot of people have missed their miracle because they first analyze God's instructions logically, rationally and based on their academic level. Please as you seek God for your financial liberty ensure you do exactly what He instructs you promptly.

Remember to return and give God thanks for the miracle (2 Kings 4:7): A wise man said that appreciation is an application for more. Every time God does a miracle for anyone He expects thanksgiving in return. Even in nature when you do something for someone you expect them to appreciate you and if they don't you may get angry and not do it for them again. In the bible book of Luke 17:17-19 Jesus heals ten lepers and only one person returned and bowed to worship Him and He said "Were there not ten cleansed but where are the nine?" That means he was expecting them to come give thanks but since they didn't return He only perfected the miracle of the person that came. Also in the case of the widow woman from our key scripture above, she returned and told the prophet how she obeyed his instructions and the result she got then the prophet told her what to do to perfect her miracle. So also you have to follow this last step because it will put a seal on your miracle and establish your financial liberty.

THE above five practical approaches are a secret that many have not discovered but because you have this book now, go ahead and act accordingly so that your miracle can be born. And when you have your miracle ensure you help others come out of debt with the light you've gotten from this book.

CONCLUSION

The path to financial freedom and a debt-free existence requires perseverance, self-control, and wise money management. Through our investigation, we have seen that while debt can be an effective instrument for advancement, if it is not handled correctly, it can also turn into an insurmountable burden.

Debt's complexity can be better understood by comprehending it in its entirety, from its historical roots to its effects on people and societies. We have examined the several types of debt, from consumer debt to government borrowing, and acknowledged the varied causes of debt that people may experience.

We must act proactively towards financial empowerment in order to overcome debt. We learn about realistic ways to get out of debt, such as the value of budgeting, prioritizing debts, haggling with creditors, and putting aside money for emergencies. With financial knowledge and a well-defined debt repayment plan, we may successfully manage the debt life-cycle and get one step closer to achieving financial independence.

But being debt-free requires more than just paying off your bills; it also calls for a change in perspective and the development of sound money management practices. Let us keep in mind to foster a culture of restraint, prudent spending, and long-term financial preparation as we work to live lives free from the chains of debt.

Even while the path to debt freedom is not without obstacles, it is unquestionably worthwhile to take. Let's be steadfast in our dedication to financial well-being as we take control of our finances and work to create a more secure and successful future for ourselves and our loved ones.

May we discover in this endeavor the fortitude to face challenges, the knowledge to make wise choices, and the fortitude to persevere. Together, we can figure out how to deal with debt's complications, take control of our financial future, and start along the road to real financial freedom and fulfillment. Let us set out on this transformational road with assurance, knowing that with commitment and tenacity, we can build a life free from debt and rich in limitless possibilities.

7 QUOTES ABOUT GETTING INTO DEBT.

"Debt is like any other trap, easy enough to get into, but hard enough to get out of."

HENRY WHEELER SHAW

"Many delight more in giving presents than in paying their debts."

SIR PHILIP SYDNEY

"Don't let your mouth write no check that your tail can't cash."

BO DIDDLEY

"Good times are when people make debts to pay in bad times."

ROBERT QUINLIN

"Some debts are fun when you are acquiring them, but none are fun when you set about retiring them."

OGDEN NASH

"Debts are like children - begot with pleasure, but brought forth with pain."

MOLIERE

"This would be a much better world if more married couples were as deeply in love as they are in debt."

EARL WILSON